Portrait of a Romance

Hip Pocket Press Mission Statement

It is our belief that the arts are the embodiment of the soul of a culture, that the promotion of writers and artists is essential if our current culture, with its emphasis on television and provocative outcomes, is to have a chance to develop that inner voice and ear that express and listen to beauty. Toward that end, Hip Pocket Press will continue to search out and discover poets and writers whose voices can give us a clearer understanding of ourselves and of the culture which defines us.

Other Books from Hip Pocket Press

You Notice the Body: Gail Rudd Entrekin (poetry)
Terrain: Dan Bellm, Molly Fisk, Forrest Hamer (poetry)
A Common Ancestor: Marilee Richards (poetry)
Sierra Songs & Descants: Poetry & Prose of the Sierra: Gail Rudd Entrekin, Ed.
Truth Be Told: Tom Farber (epigrams)
Songs for a Teenage Nomad: Kim Culbertson (Young Adult fiction)
Yuba Flows: Kirsten Casey, Gary Cooke, Cheryl Dumesnil, Judy Halebsky, Iven Lourie & Scott Young; Gail Rudd Entrekin, Ed. (poetry)
The More Difficult Beauty: Molly Fisk (poetry)
Ex Vivo (Out of the Living Body): Kirsten Casey (poetry)
Even That Indigo: John Smith (poetry)
The Berkeley Poets Cooperative: A History of the Times: Charles Entrekin, Ed. (essays)
Jester: Grace Marie Grafton (poetry)

Web Publications
Canary, a Literary Journal of the Environmental Crisis:
www.hippocketpress.org/canary.cfm
Sisyphus, Essays on Language, Culture & the Arts:
www.hippocketpress.org/sisyphus.cfm

Portrait of a Romance

Charles Entrekin

Orinda, CA
2014

Published by Hip Pocket Press
5 Del Mar Court
Orinda, CA 94563
www.hippocketpress.org

This edition was produced for on-demand distribution by lightningsource.com for Hip Pocket Press.

Typesetting: Wordsworth of Marin (wordsworthofmarin.com)
Typeface: Comic Sans
Cover Art & Design: LeeAnn Brook (brookdesign.com)
Cover Photo: Charles Entrekin (Berkeley, CA)
Artwork: Ross Drago
Italicized Quotations: Coleman Barks translations of thirteenth century Persian poet Jalāl ad-Dīn Muhammad Rūmī

Acknowledgment: This book could not have been produced without the able assistance of Heidi Varian, who assisted in all stages of its production.

Copyright © 2014 by Charles Entrekin

No part of this book may be reproduced or transmitted in any form or by any means, graphic, electronic or mechanical, including photocopying, recording, taping or by any information storage or retrieval system, without permission in writing from the publisher.

Printed in the United States of America.

ISBN 0-917658-43-4
ISBN 13: 978-0-917658-43-3

For Gail

"...we have ways within each other
that will never be said by anyone."

—Rumi

Contents

Prelude

    Seeking Safety   13
    Artwork 1   14

Eros: Desire

    Under the Pyramid Building   17
    Discovered   18
    Fragments from Nine Months   19
    In My Museum of Afternoons   22
    September   23
    Russian River   24
    Artwork 2   25
    Hold Me   26
    Sex, Genetics, the Sea   28
    Artwork 3   30

Aphrodisia: Passion

    In This Hour   33
    Point Pinole   34
    Letting Go   35
    We Dance   36
    No Reason   37

Fort Mason Bar, San Francisco   38
Inside Us   39
Artwork 4   40

Pragma: Lasting Love

Fishing   43
Tuggle Road Exit   45
Yuba River Time   46
Artwork 5   47
Fear of Falling   48
Wife   50
An Early Morning Surprise   51
Watching You Undress   52
Sonata of the Plastic Curtain   54
Artwork 6   56

Agape: Selfless Love

Dana Street, Berkeley, CA   59
November in Berkeley   60
Artwork 7   61
Snapshots   62
For Gail on Her 66th Birthday   64

Prelude

*"Stop the words now.
Open the window in the center of your chest,
and let the words fly in and out."*

—Rumi

Seeking Safety

Even as a little girl, she was petite and pretty but pragmatic, a birthright of organizational ability given to her by her mother. Her father gave her the gift of adventure, and freedom from conventional wisdom. So of course her first lover took her to the brink of discovery in her first full pleasure of touch, but the chasm of ongoing miscommunications grew. Soon she knew she would have to start over. So she left him. Divorced him. Went back to school. After her MA, she tried an artist, a photographer who created nude faceless bodies in black and white. No commitments, jealousy, great sex, and no future. Next was a run of aloneness and bad dreams of failure. Sitting in a dark closet, alone, seemed appropriate. Only poetry seemed possible. The rest was stress and emptiness. She was ready to settle down, and then she met me.

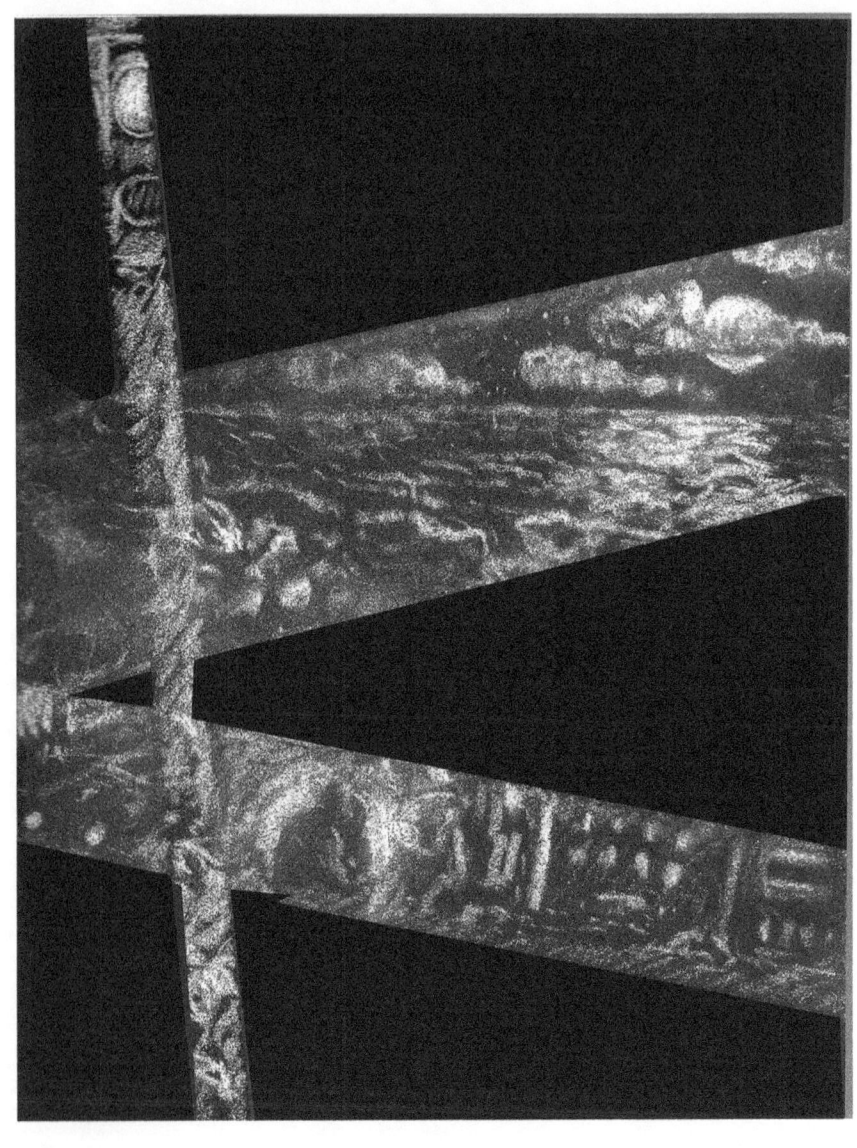

EROS: Desire

"Out beyond the ideas of wrongdoing and rightdoing, there is a field. I'll meet you there."

—Rumi

Under the Pyramid Building

We were
as in a movie;
I kissed her,

ran my fingers under her dress,
touched her with the tip of my tongue,
kissed her

with my fingertips
as a cab driver looked on

the wet pavement, umbrellas and raincoats,
and lovers,

standing there off Broadway,
folded into one another, become
slow moving as statues in the rain,

creatures clumsily awakening,
as if lifting upwards out of stone.

Discovered

Honeysuckle, family Caprifoliaceous,
delicate
yellow and white tubular petals,
green-thick vines, and
hummingbirds at rest
in still-flight, with
sharp red and violet breasts.

Like the vine,
your glance
entangling,
everywhere I look,
your face.

Fragments from Nine Months, 1981

January

sometimes we try
to give away
what we most need
of ourselves

February

all weekend I have been filled
with a kind of emotional white light
like going snow blind suddenly
I become abstracted
remember your eyes
afterwards
sit and remain silent

March

I find you now inside me
like a note in a bottle
a silver jar filled with sadness
a place to return to
of knowing and not knowing
your red hair and brown eyes
sudden implacabilities there

April

beside the Great Highway
a night orange fire in the distance
dancing inside me
refusing to die down

May

tonight I feel the sea
reclaiming the land little by little
I stand on shifting ground
we are walking in sand
something I want but cannot have
gets dispersed in a cold wet wind

June

pink
round and touching smooth
I want to preserve each
first time
entering you

July

I was talking to the wind today
about disorder and
songs that have no sound
about your eyes
and what's in them
about waves and wet sand
and never explaining

August

outside Hayfork
beside two coyotes
hanging upside down from a farmer's fence
butterflies rise around my boots
a narrow creek clatters over rocks

September

out an old Victorian window
yellow curtains are flowing
as I'm leaving
I'm startled to remember
my hand drifting
over your bare shoulder
and back

In My Museum of Afternoons

      We are crossing barbed wire
leaving childhood behind
stepping over rotted-out posts
of memory.
      Hazy green dream
of deer droppings in a Pacific meadow
surf echoing offshore
occasional barking of a seal
whisper of wisps of sea fog.
      Now I am with you,
holding your hand, and we are new
in beginning the pleasures
of our being alone, together.
      Edging above sea and sky
a white moon mask revels
through rushing black clouds
a dance of reveal and go.
      Behind us was the wind
we breathed in, and we are alive
dancing in the touch and the smell
of each other's skin.

September

      In you, tonight, I felt your emptiness,
and yes, I wanted to pour myself
inside it, my hands in your life,
      how it was as we ran the paths
in the park, the dahlias all in bloom,
dusky red, yellow, like flesh
at the center,
      and when we spoke of broken things,
and you said, touch me, hold me,
and I did.

Russian River

      How is it we come to this?
She sits poised at the edge, the boat
ribbed in shadows. She speaks of trust.
I talk of what remains.
      Autumn and the glare off the water
lights her red hair. She sits unruffled
and calm, while something I wanted,
and awkwardly am, begins to spin
inside me.
      I say I am not afraid, but I am.
I have let the boat drift. And as her breath
moves across my neck, a strange feeling rushes
through me, searching for a place to rest,
and I have been waiting a long time
without knowing it.

Hold Me

Out the window the land falls away into gray
bay and boats with furled sails,
a foggy winter's day on the Mendocino Coast.
And then, just flushed from lovemaking,
all red in your plum-like soul,
you ask, still wet and glistening,
if I love you.

Side by side, our bodies still touch.
Kelp beds are bobbing in the surf,
and for a long moment afterwards
I slip back into myself, my historical
self, and remember them

my first wife in bed
trying a guitar chord
she never quite mastered,

and my second wife
standing alone in her door,
empty as a silvery abalone shell,

and suddenly I feel the cold
as rain and wind begin to lash
the highway home. Hold me,
I say, watching the waves pound,
and raindrops streaking down
the glass.

Sex, Genetics, the Sea

Like falling backwards in time
toward something I don't comprehend,
    if I stand still
    if I run forward
that what I see has no name,
slouches away if I look at it,
yet feel in the touch of bones
    in what has gone before,
as if it were a story, like coming home
and finding each other alone while
    a heavy wet log lifts and falls,
    lifts and falls. And with each soughing
the ground shakes, and I need to know more
of the rumpled shapes of our dreaming out loud
together, of the coming storms, the wind
already stirring the curtains,
    of the rising and falling, asymmetrically
falling over your wet-tongued ear,
a seascape of white sky,
a shoreline of succulents,
of iceplants,
    and I can see you still,
eyes dazzled in the daylight,
face washed red beside the sluiced
rock slide,

and the waiting engines of our lives
start forward again, like heavy ships at sea
that can turn only a little at a time,
      creating what we are, the moment
of penetration, of entering another's life,
of losing one's own.

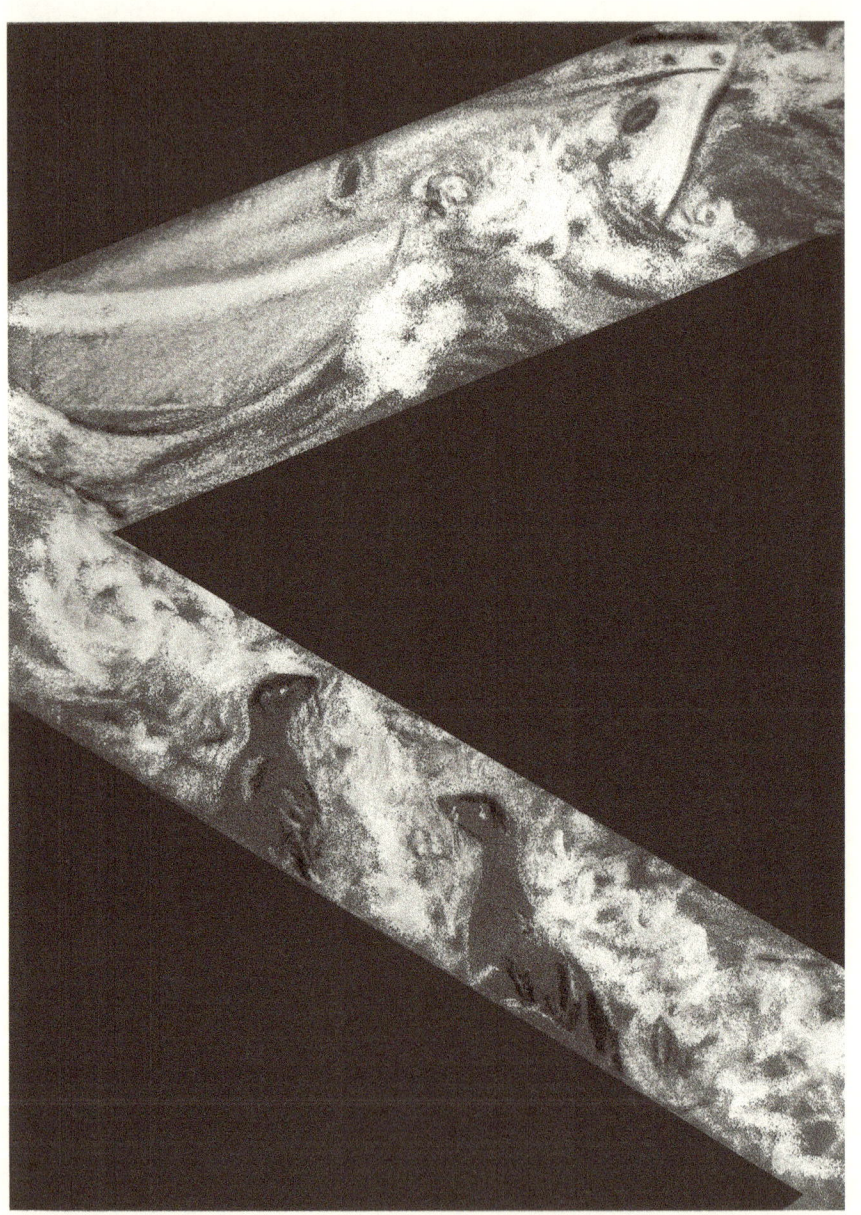

APHRODISIA: Passion

"...the world is too full to talk about.
Ideas, language, even the phrase each other
doesn't make any sense."

—*Rumi*

In This Hour

Even in the fog and dark wind
I can feel the tide coming in,
the steady wash and swell,
and sea salt along the shore,
and I try to make myself empty
to no avail.
   Somewhere ahead I imagine
an avenging angel, one of swift
shadow and sure ending, and I can
almost feel its beating wings,
a predator breaking from cover
in full autumn sail.
   But for now, in this hour,
the sea's lapping continues and
it's like an animal breathing
against the beach. I listen with each
light touch of the surf, and my hand
moves inside your silence, inside
your life and body's warmth.

Point Pinole

Lying in sunlight, I know her like a memory,
eyes closed, freshly
fallen, veins and dreams over her eyelids.
I stare into Eucalyptus leaves, watch
two black fishermen hold up their catch
to one another. In the distance
behind the Golden Gate, the sun
casts everything in pink. In a few minutes
we will leave. Nothing will be the same.

A barge creeps across the skyline.
She sits up, legs straight out like a child,
and I see beyond her, almost breaking,
the top branches caught in the heavy wind,
bending something inside me, and yes,
this is what follows, these winds
blowing always from the same direction,
from what we leave behind,
a reality of mornings,
of one day after another,
of keeping safe in a safe house.

Letting Go

Yes. Best of all is the water, flat,
skipping stones on the surface. Empty
evening light. Yes. It was perfect.
We made love and napped in the firelight.
Outside, the gray breath of a storm.
I remember bluegill, fish large
as your hand, swimming like leaves,
and my grandfather's bottom land,
his swamps and creeks. Yes,
your breasts remember me, and
my fingers remember you,
soft as chrysanthemums, wet.
Yes. All right. But afterwards
when I said never mind the old man
in the restaurant with money,
never mind the cold incoming fog,
it made no difference.
Yes. I know each evening
brings the chance of being wrong,
but tonight the water's smooth, and
even in December the sea birds are here,
arriving in a vague and brittle white
across the sea shore; they are on time
and alive inside their own complex
of reasons and joy.

We Dance

Leaning back
you press your pubic bone
up against my hand,
a soft nuzzling motion,
then stop, elbows up, head back.
And I smile into the soft
flesh over hip bone,
the warm wet feel of you
on my fingertips.
We dance.

No Reason

but the red comes with the flush of her
sweet bold breath, with her touch,
the playful tip of her tongue

and then the sudden heat beneath
her skirt, and the wet feel
my fingers reveal, explore,

my soul leaning in, suddenly
naked and surrendering, afloat
in the salt-sea of her season.

Fort Mason Bar, San Francisco

      She smiles just like before,
but not the same, the same but arriving
from a great distance. A storm's
heavy waves wash the wet dark pier
before us. I nurse a hot brandy.
Steam gathers in my glass.
      It's that she leans into me now
with her smile, somehow centered forward,
a new lever and fulcrum balanced within
her, a new seed centering her universe.
      And even as I see it in her,
I want to say, *Let's go now*, but I don't.
Something remains sleeping within me,
a dream I haven't reasoned out,
and so we sit, time holding us suspended
like seals in the sea before us,
unable to go home.

Inside Us

A dark pool at night,
two animals drinking
alone, standing
shoulder to shoulder
together.

PRAGMA: Enduring Love

"Come to the orchard in Spring.
There will be light and wine, and sweethearts
in the pomegranate flowers.
If you do not come, these do not matter.
If you do come, these do not matter."

—Rumi

Fishing

Fishing for brim,
a delicate bony fish,
one must go slow,
move with the trees.

A formal activity, yet
it's full of surprises;
we could lie down on the bank,
take off our clothes,
make love in the mud.

Personally, I don't think you'd like
the fishing part, but you'd come anyway,
to watch me, childlike in my thickness,
all wet and matching wits
with the underworld.

But have you ever noticed how color works
with cows in the woods? They blend in,
become tricky creatures suddenly,
try to hook you if they can, explode
out of nowhere, become docile again.

It's how we are with ourselves,
me especially, enthralled in a mood
I can't control, and I don't give in
easily. But under an empty sky with you
we can try for bluegill, some large
as my hand, and they're leapers, fighters,
dappled as the freckles on your thigh.

Tuggle Road Exit

Sunday, leaving the airport,
we decide to stop to eat,
find a shopping center.
We park in the only empty slot
across from WalMart.
Low clouds glower in reflected light.
Rain threatens.

New cars whiz by us,
Hummers,
Chryslers,
Dodge minivans,
Jeep Cherokees.

We stand under a closed gray sky
when I take your hand and begin
to cross against traffic,
and suddenly have to run for it.
And as your warm fingers
interlock with mine, I am not surprised
at how we begin to glow,
how we are both flushed with heat signal,
how I know that we are the only ones left alive
who have escaped once more
in this landscape of concrete and cars.

Yuba River Time

Sunlit, what's left behind from 1849,
the slurry running over granite for years
'til the Yuba's silt-smoothed stones
gather heat in the summer sun

and the lovers return
for the rocks' offering
of warmth, curves matching her hips,
support for the bones of her back,

and hands take him into
her softest parts
spread open and wet
as the Yuba rushes past

the blackberry vines,
the understory of oaks,
the lovers amongst the rocks,
and the crash and the detritus of thought
are washed away.

Fear of Falling

        There isn't much.
I'm here, thinking of you
late in the afternoon, before sunset,
watching a mist of cloud rise toward me
up the South Yuba River Canyon.
As it blocks out the orderly fir forest below,
the sun falters, and the pink penetrating light of day
disappears in a thick fog of rain, palpably gray.

        Then it comes back to me,
about last night's dream of almost falling,
of standing in a strong wind
precariously balanced
on a disappearing ledge and
shouting at people fleeing below
about which way to go.

      Yesterday was fraught
with pain. Hard decisions.
But as we lay down naked and
folded ourselves into one another
on our Tuesday afternoon in the rain,
I let it all go, because
I knew I could rise with you, up
over our canyon where, like hawks
who have found how to mate in mid-air,
I knew I could enter you
and have no fear of falling.

Wife

Last night, naked and alive
in our skin, we lay nuzzling in
side by side, joining,
coming together in the wet
heat of our flesh,
      and all day I know
the damp feel of your heavy
auburn hair, and the pink glow of your face
as, eyes closed, you pull your hips forward
over me,
      feel how it is right,
this surface tension and touching
we create, fingertips across
each other's skin like water striders
until the punctured surface gives in,
and we begin with the long fall inside
one another.

An Early Morning Surprise

Prances about in her new pink panties
wearing her young girl's smile,
teasing me with liquid amber eyes,
with arms held high in play,
a butterfly mood holding her in sway,

and then self-consciousness sets in
as she stands in her freckles
and pale white skin
quite embarrassed
and a rose-red blush
spreads over both her breasts,
the eager one and the recalcitrant one,

and I rush to embrace her fun,
her playful dance and display
I will carry with me all day.

Watching You Undress

Tonight, watching you undress was
like falling backwards in time
toward that moment in our past when
      it became clear to me
      that nothing would ever be the same.
I had stepped over the line.
Everything would be redefined.
My past life slipped away, and
what mattered was the new reality that
arrived with the touch of your bones,
      and my new world, my interior life
remained only a story about to be told,
and so suddenly I needed to know more
about the rumpled shapes
of our dreaming out loud together

because I knew about the coming storms,
the wind already stirring the curtains, and I could see
the cumulus clouds gathering around you,
because you had stopped and turned,
because you lay down under me as I entered
into your warmth, your eyes opened wide,
because in that first moment of penetration
before my hands reached into your life, I knew
there was only one path forward, knew it
before our children were born, knew it before
the waterfall of our decisions had swept us
into this future.
    And I stopped to watch you undress.

Sonata of the Plastic Curtain

As each hook snaps loose,
its plastic shape exploding toward the ceiling,
you think *maybe this is not happening*
as you feel yourself falling,
your feet slipping out from under, and you
think, *but why now*,
hands flailing, seeing
your naked wife's body
float away in soap suds
and shower spray,
her soft rosy breasts, soapy hands,
large wide brown eyes watching
as you fall backwards from the tub
as from an airplane, the slapping sound
of water striking the disappearing wall
while your hands are busy grasping at nothing
and the sonata of the plastic curtain
reverberates around you as the hooks,
in staccato bursts, blast into space,
and you think *maybe this is not real*,

just before you hit the floor,
before the porcelain toilet
slams against your shoulder,
and the music stops,
almost as if someone
turned off the car radio
leaving you with the traffic,
the humming of an engine,
and someplace else you need to go.

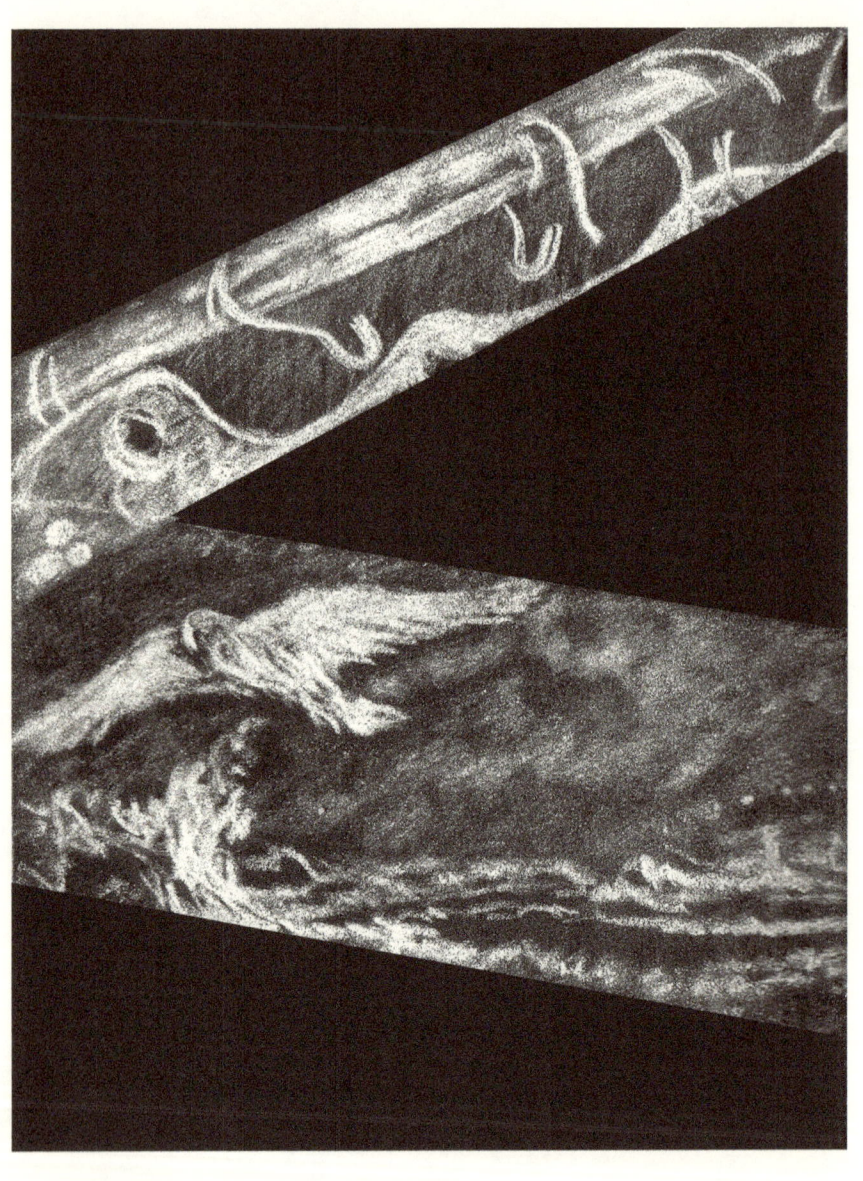

AGAPE: Selfless Love

"Don't worry about saving these songs!
And if one of our instruments breaks,
it doesn't matter.
We have fallen into the place
where everything is music."

—Rumi

Dana Street, Berkeley, CA

      As I climb the stairs behind you,
your freckled shoulders droop beneath your blouse.
With the dishes washed and the children asleep,
we've turned our attention to tomorrow.
      I place both hands on your hips,
cup cheeks with a squeeze, push,
lift your bottom to help you up the stairs,
enjoy the slippery feel of you
in new white pants.
      Later, in bed, we listen
to the sudden rain and an early winter wind
bringing threats of breakage into our tree-top room,
but we are not afraid because we can hear in it our song,
our wind chime, a Woodstock, as it keeps its melody
whole even as it swings in the wind dancing
frantically to and fro, releasing wild tubular cymbals
harmonic, pentatonic scales, a feast for our ears,
a fairyland of fanning branches swooshing all around us,
as we curl up in each other's arms, safe,
grateful to have found one another at last, able
to make love in the beauty of storms.

November in Berkeley

      The back door,
hanging by its heels,
swings open
and it's November again.
      Outside, pittosporum berries,
orange and whiskey-scented,
have fallen to the ground.
But there will be no snow,
no bears in the driveway,
and no frozen pond, its murky waters
gone veined and milky as glass.
      It's good the way we invent what we need,
catering our lives with beginnings and endings,
the way I look backwards wearing disasters
on my sleeve, and you, planning ahead,
search for joy in every potted plant, and
it's as if here,
where winter never really comes,
      we have learned
to rely on our inner clocks
and let the seasons
reach inch-by-inch
into the soil of ourselves.

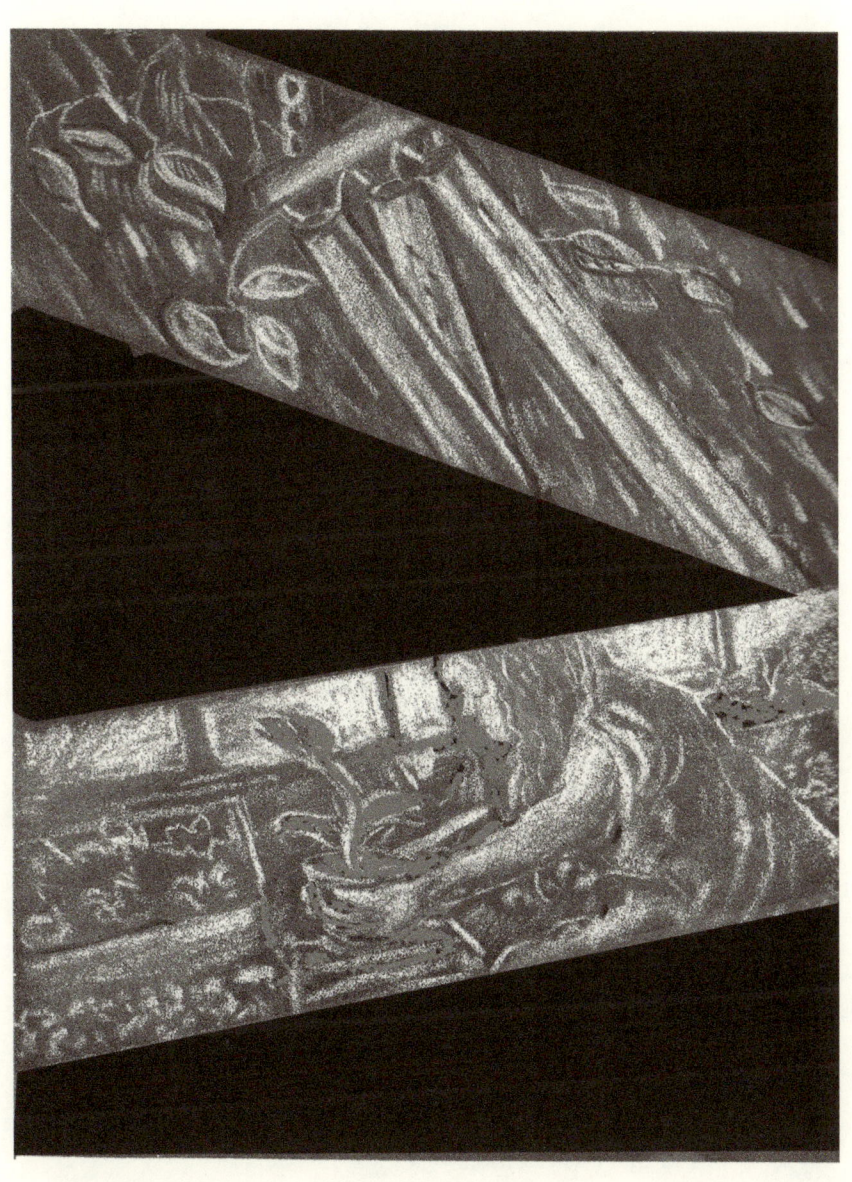

Snapshots
after a poem by Pablo Neruda

Naked you are
in transparent skin,
rose-colored breasts, curly mons veneris,
mischievously posing, you are
a wood nymph in the cottonwoods
at Clear Lake.

Naked, we have taken ecstasy
at Howard Creek Ranch, and your openings
are mauve as foxglove. You are lying back in ocean light,
in the rising and falling of sea sounds, and
I am entering in through the pores of your skin.

Naked you are lying back in the tub
on Sonoma Street, your great baby belly before you.
Nathan, inside you, rolls over, whale-like, shows us his foot.
With your great blue-veined breasts lolling pink
above the white suds, you are helpless to move.
Your wry smile floats up to me. You are
overwhelmingly in flower.

Naked in our Sierras, in winter, you are a small flame
against the cold room around us.
Shivering, I reach out for you,
snuggle into the flowing heat of you, place
my hands in the warm nest of your hair.
You are my familiar, my lover, my wife.

For Gail on her 66th Birthday

       We were still in our first days together,
when a wild poet named David Fisher,
as if sharing a secret,
fixed me with an intent look of madness,
and whispered, "I saw her first.
She was out there in the world
all by herself, Ms. Gail Rudd.
But she didn't want me.
So now I see who it will be:
you will be the one."
       And I am the one.
I am the one who loves this woman
this multi-tasker, master planner,
this beautiful poet
striving for clarity, this woman who
alphabetizes all our books
by subject and author,
who always keeps our canned goods
facing front.
       I'm the one who loves her
as she turns on the stove and walks away,
leaving the pan unattended,
tomato soup boiling over,
while she answers an e-mail
or reads a new poem,
or designs her latest Kandinsky quilt.

    She loves her lacy black underwear,
and, yes, I love her for that,
and, yes, she takes risks:
she always believes she can make it
and occasionally runs red lights.
    I love her because
she has a generous, plum-like soul.
She loves to figure out
the etymology of words,
because she loves children, animals, and birds,
and because I was the one.

www.ingramcontent.com/pod-product-compliance
Lightning Source LLC
Chambersburg PA
CBHW020959090426
42736CB00010B/1387